Educators Love STEP-UP Books.
So Do Children.*

In this exciting series:

- THE WORDS ARE HARDER (but not too hard)
- THERE'S A LOT MORE TEXT (but it's in bigger print)
- THERE ARE PLENTY OF ILLUSTRATIONS (but they are not just picture books)
- And the subject matter has been carefully chosen to appeal to young readers who want to find out about the world for themselves. These informative and lively books are just the answer.

*"STEP-UP BOOKS

. . . fill a need for precise informational material written in a simple readable form which children can and will enjoy. More please!"—EVELYN L. HEADLEY, *Director of Elementary Education, Edison, New Jersey.*

"I love them."—STEVE MEYER, *second grade pupil, Chicago, Illinois.*

For
My Mother and Father
Love, MKF

PREHISTORIC MONSTERS

did the

STRANGEST

THINGS

by

Leonora and Arthur Hornblow

illustrated by Michael K. Frith

Step-Up Books — Random House

New York

Library of Congress Cataloging in Publication Data: Hornblow, Leonora. Prehistoric monsters did the strangest things. (Step-up books, no. 23) SUMMARY: Briefly describes, in chronological order, many of the strange animals that lived on earth between the time life began and the appearance of man. 1. Vertebrates. Fossil—Juvenile literature [1. Prehistoric animals. 2. Fossils] I. Hornblow, Arthur, joint author. II. Frith, Michael K., illus. III. Title. QE842.H67 566 73-9348 ISBN 0-394-82051-7 ISBN 0-394-92051-1 (lib. bdg.)

Contents

The Ball of Fire

Billions and billions of years ago
there were no people. There were
no animals. There were no trees or
flowers. Our earth was made of gases
and stardust. It was a huge ball of
fire. No one is sure how this fire
began. But it burned all the time.

The earth kept on burning inside. But after billions of years the outside began to cool off. It started to crack. Boiling mud and hot rock gushed out. Clouds of steam hung over the earth. The clouds turned to rain. Water was everywhere. Now life on the earth could begin.

The Wet Ones

Life began in the water. The water then was warm and salty. The air was hot and damp. Little plants began to grow. Soon, small creatures started to crawl on the bottom of the sea.

After a long time, some of these strange crawlers turned into fish. At first they were very small. Over many, many years some kinds of fish grew larger and larger.

Some fish became sharks. There are still sharks in the sea today. Some sharks now are bigger than those sharks of millions of years ago. But they are still the same in many ways. Their bodies are covered with thousands of scales. These are like tiny teeth. Their mouths are filled with real teeth. They are fierce and hungry fish. That is the way sharks have always been. It is strange that they have changed so little—and the world has changed so much.

Land-Ho!

For millions of years, every creature lived in the sea. Slowly, as time went on, rocks and sand rose out of the water. Some sea creatures crawled up on this land. One of the early crawlers was strange-looking Diplocaulus (dip-lo-CALL-us). He had such an odd head. It looked like an arrow! But Diplocaulus couldn't stay long on land. His legs were small and very weak. He could not crawl far. He had to go back into the water to find food.

The Seymouria (see-MOOR-ee-uh)
spent most of his time on land. He was
a small creature. His legs were strong,
so he was able to crawl far from the sea.
He looked for plants and insects to eat.
The air was cooler than it had been
and more plants were growing. Many
insects were living among the plants.
So little Seymouria could choose a
tasty dinner.

Sunny Side Out

Dimetrodon (dye-MET-ro-don)
lived on land all the time.
He was a reptile. There are
still reptiles on earth. But
nothing like a Dimetrodon!
Dimetrodon had
lots of teeth. Some
teeth were large
and some were small.
But they all were sharp.
Dimetrodon needed them
because he did not eat
plants. This reptile
ate other reptiles.

The strangest thing about
Dimetrodon was the piece of
skin on his back. It looked
like a sail. But he did not use
it as a sail. It did not help him
move faster. He probably used
his "sail" to help keep him
warm. When he felt cold he
would turn sideways. Then his
"sail" would soak up the sun's
heat. Lucky Dimetrodon.
He had his own
built-in heater.

The Magic Eyes

Some reptiles lived in the water all the time. Ichthyosaur (ICK-thee-o-sore) was one of these. He looked like a big fish, but he was really a reptile. He ate other sea creatures. He dove down deep to hunt for food. Ichthyosaur was a fierce hunter. He had long, cruel jaws and as many as 200 sharp teeth.

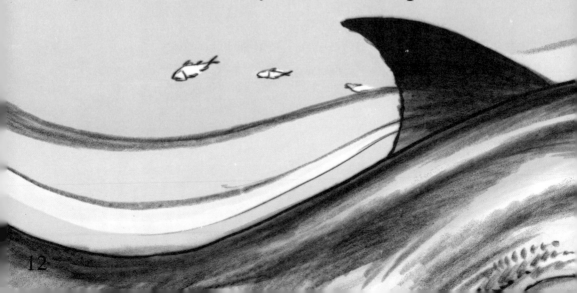

Around his eyes the Ichthyosaur had rings of bone. These bony rings could become larger or smaller. This may have helped him see better in the dark water. And when he dove the rings got smaller. This kept the water from pressing against his eyes. A strange trick to us, but an easy one for an Ichthyosaur.

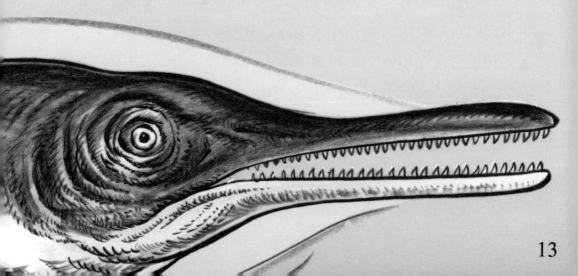

What Mary Found

Only a little over a hundred years ago,
an English girl named Mary Anning
was looking for sea shells. She found
the bones of an Ichthyosaur! Scientists
were very excited—all the Ichthyosaurs
had been dead for millions of years.
Since Mary, many people in many places
have dug up the bones of other monsters.
Putting the bones together is like doing
jigsaw puzzles. And people have found
animal footprints and outlines of plants
from millions of years ago. Over the
years these had turned to stone. These
bones and outlines are called fossils.

Fossils are very important. They help
us learn about the earliest animals.
These animals lived millions of years
before there were any people. There
was no one to write about them. There
was no one to draw their pictures.
Fossils are the only way we know about
these prehistoric monsters. There are
fossils and bones in many museums. If
you visit them, remember Mary Anning
. . . and what she found.

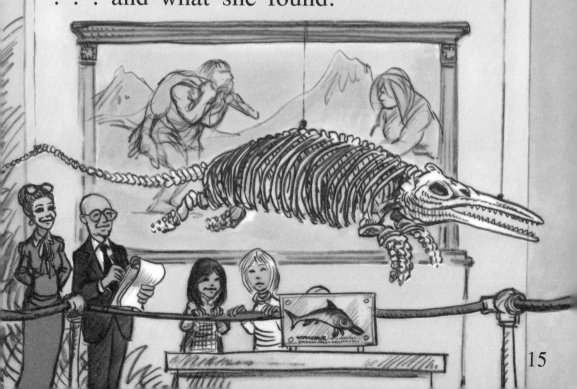

Here Come the Dinosaurs

In prehistoric times the land was almost always changing. Great mountains rose where there were no mountains before. And there were new lakes and deserts. The air was hot and dry. The reptiles liked this heat. They grew bigger and stronger. It was a good time for reptiles.

A new kind of reptile was roaming the earth—the Dinosaur (DIE-no-sore). Dinosaur means "terrible lizard." Many dinosaurs were terrible; all dinosaurs were strange. For millions of years they were the rulers of the world.

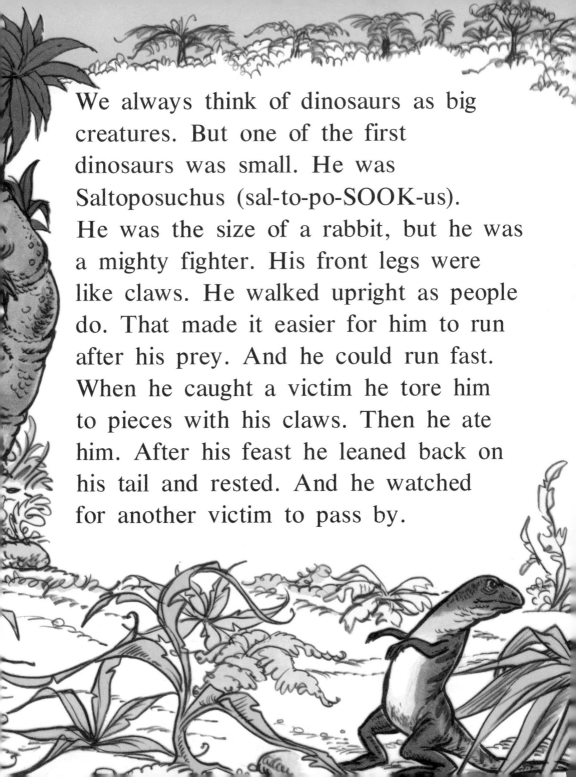

We always think of dinosaurs as big
creatures. But one of the first
dinosaurs was small. He was
Saltoposuchus (sal-to-po-SOOK-us).
He was the size of a rabbit, but he was
a mighty fighter. His front legs were
like claws. He walked upright as people
do. That made it easier for him to run
after his prey. And he could run fast.
When he caught a victim he tore him
to pieces with his claws. Then he ate
him. After his feast he leaned back on
his tail and rested. And he watched
for another victim to pass by.

Giants

One of the biggest dinosaurs was
Brontosaurus (bron-to-SORE-us).
He was almost 80 feet long. He
weighed about 60,000 pounds.
When he walked his footsteps
must have sounded like thunder.
His name means "thunder lizard."
For all his great size he had
a tiny brain. So huge
Brontosaurus was
terribly dumb.

Brontosaurus was a land
animal. But he spent most
of his time in the water.
He ate the plants that
grew there. Every
day he ate tons of
plants.

It took
a lot of
plants to
fill that
huge stomach.
But there was an even
bigger dinosaur. This
was Brachiosaurus.

19

The biggest dinosaur that ever lived was Brachiosaurus (BRAKE-ee-o-sore-us). Many dinosaurs had short weak front legs. Brachiosaurus had big strong legs. But he was so heavy, it was hard for him to walk. It was easier to move in the water. He ate water plants. He never ate meat. But the meat-eating dinosaurs wanted to eat him.

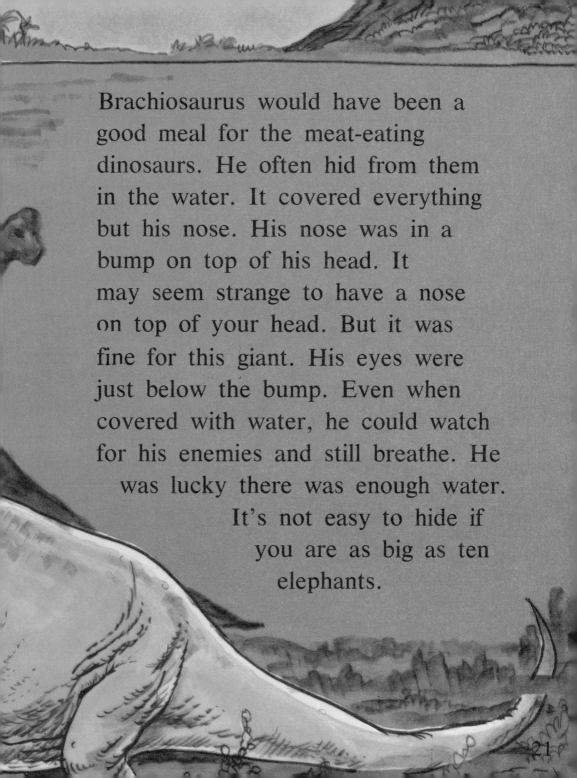

Brachiosaurus would have been a
good meal for the meat-eating
dinosaurs. He often hid from them
in the water. It covered everything
but his nose. His nose was in a
bump on top of his head. It
may seem strange to have a nose
on top of your head. But it was
fine for this giant. His eyes were
just below the bump. Even when
covered with water, he could watch
for his enemies and still breathe. He
was lucky there was enough water.
It's not easy to hide if
you are as big as ten
elephants.

The Terrible Tail

Some of the dinosaurs did not have to hide in the water. The Stegosaurus (STEG-o-sore-us) did not hide anywhere. He didn't need to. He was very well covered. It was hard for his enemies to get at him. He had two rows of tough horn on his back and tail. At the end of his tail there were four sharp spikes.

Stegosaurus had a very tiny brain. He was so stupid, he needed help. So he had a kind of second brain where his tail began. This "second brain" could warn him of danger. Then he would lash out with his spiked tail. When he was left alone, Stegosaurus was peaceful. He ate plants. He liked cactus best of all. Most of the time the meat-eating dinosaurs probably left him alone. Maybe they were afraid of the terrible tail with a "mind" of its own.

Up and Away

There were reptiles on land. There
were reptiles in the sea. And now there
were reptiles in the air. One of these
was Rhamphorhynchus (ram-fo-RINK-us).
He was a glider. He had a piece of skin
that stretched from his front legs to
his back claws. He could lift this to
catch the wind. Then he would float in
the air like a little kite. At the tip of
his long tail he had a flap of skin.
It helped him to steer. The reptile
that got off the ground must have been
a strange sight.

About the time Rhamphorhynchus was gliding, another strange creature was really flying. He was Archaeopteryx (ar-kee-OP-ter-ix). He had the beak and feathers of a bird, but the teeth of a reptile. He could not stay up in the air very long. Luckily for him, he had claws on his wings. When he wanted to rest he could grab onto a rock or a tree. He never flew very far. But the odd Archaeopteryx was our world's first flyer with feathers.

The Frilly Monster

The world was still changing. The air
was cooler. More trees and more plants
were growing. And there were flowers
now. This was the time of the strangest
dinosaurs of all. One of them was
Styracosaurus (sty-RAK-o-sore-us).
He had huge horns on his head. They
made him look fierce. But he used them
only to defend himself. If he was left
alone, he was a peaceful dinosaur. He
did not have to kill animals for food.
He only ate plants. His teeth worked
like scissors. They cut the plants. If
one tooth fell out he always had another
one growing under it. Styracosaurus
could keep right on eating.

Around his neck Styracosaurus had a
frill. It was made of six sharp spikes.
That made it hard for an enemy to bite
the back of his neck. Styracosaurus
was born with his frill. It grew as he
did. And he grew to be very heavy. He
was too heavy to walk upright as many
dinosaurs did. The frilly monster just
clumped along on his four thick legs.

The Odd-Bills

Imagine a dinosaur with a bill like a duck! That sounds strange, but there were many kinds of duck-bill dinosaurs. They lived both on land and in the water. Most duck-bills had odd crests of bone on top of their heads. Some crests were shaped like feathers. Some looked like helmets, others like ax blades. These strange crests stored air. The duck-bills were able to stay under water longer because of the extra air.

The duck-bills were good swimmers.
Their toes were webbed like a duck's.
This helped them move through the
water. None of the duck-bills had a
shell or tough skin. It would have
been easy for their enemies to hurt
them. So, if they were attacked, they
tried to hide in the water. When their
enemies went away, the duck-bills came
back on land. Then they could have
dinner—some fresh green plants.

The Snap and the Gulp

Elasmosaurus (ee-laz-mo-SORE-us)
spent all his time in the sea. He was a
very long creature. And he had strong
paddle legs. Every day he slowly rowed
himself through the water with his
legs. He could even row backwards! He
looked for fish to eat. When he saw a
fish, out went his long neck. His
strong jaws took hold of the fish. Snap!
His mouth closed over it. And that was
the end of the fish.

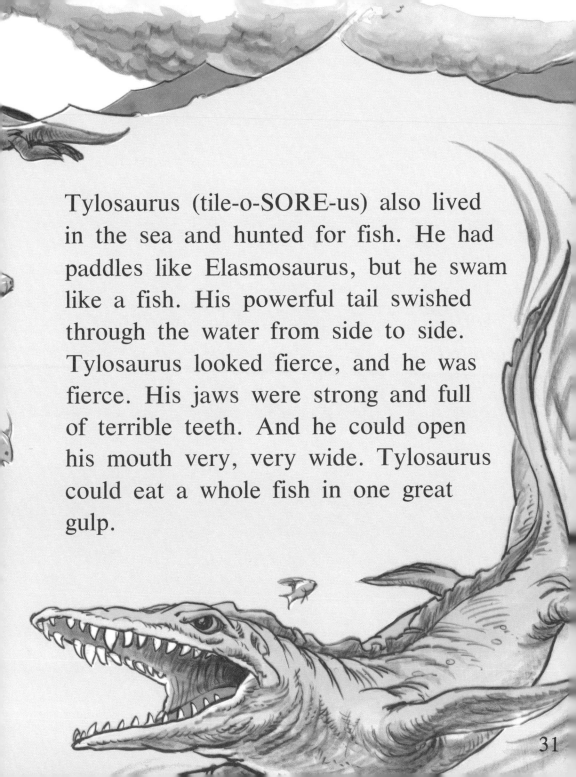

Tylosaurus (tile-o-SORE-us) also lived in the sea and hunted for fish. He had paddles like Elasmosaurus, but he swam like a fish. His powerful tail swished through the water from side to side. Tylosaurus looked fierce, and he was fierce. His jaws were strong and full of terrible teeth. And he could open his mouth very, very wide. Tylosaurus could eat a whole fish in one great gulp.

The Swimming House

The first turtles lived on land. So did many of their later relatives. But after millions of years some turtles moved into the water. Each new family of turtles grew bigger and bigger. At last the biggest turtles of all appeared. They were Archelons (ARK-uh-lons). They looked like turtles we might meet now, except for their great size.

An Archelon was as big as a car! These giants lived to be over a hundred years old. Turtles of today also live for many years. One reason is, they can live for some time without food. Another reason is, they carry their own shelters—the shells on their backs. These shell "houses" keep them safe from their enemies. And no turtle is ever very far from home.

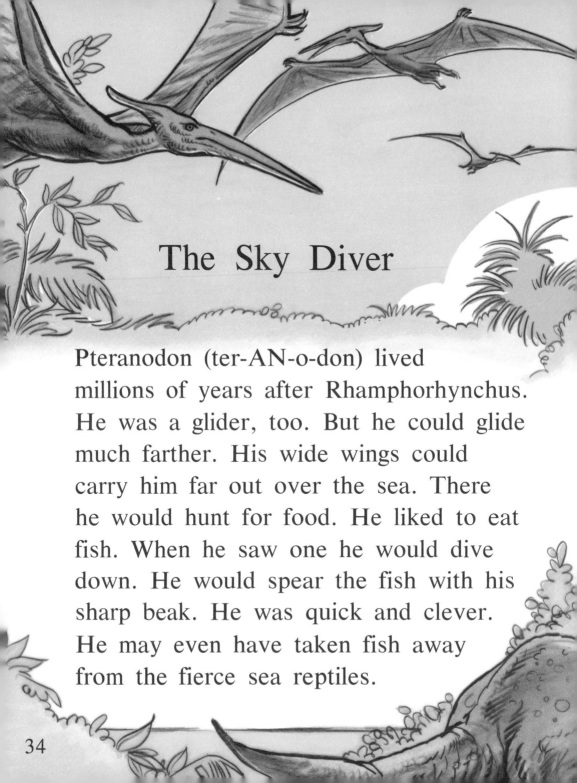

The Sky Diver

Pteranodon (ter-AN-o-don) lived
millions of years after Rhamphorhynchus.
He was a glider, too. But he could glide
much farther. His wide wings could
carry him far out over the sea. There
he would hunt for food. He liked to eat
fish. When he saw one he would dive
down. He would spear the fish with his
sharp beak. He was quick and clever.
He may even have taken fish away
from the fierce sea reptiles.

Good-by Dinosaurs

The last and the largest of the meat-eating dinosaurs was Tyrannosaurus Rex (tie-RAN-o-sore-us). He was strong and he was cruel. He tried to kill and eat every creature he met. And every creature was afraid of him. Only the horned dinosaurs like Styracosaurus would dare to fight with him. But even their horns did not help much against the terrible Tyrannosaurus.

Tyrannosaurus walked upright. His
front legs were short and weak. He
never used them. But his back legs
were long and strong. He would jump
out at his prey. He would attack them
with his teeth. He had rows and rows
of sharp teeth in his huge mouth. He
would tear his prey apart. He didn't
need strong front legs as long as
he had those awful teeth.

"Rex" means "king." Tyrannosaurus Rex was the king of his world. But his world was coming to an end. All the land dinosaurs were dying. Flying and swimming reptiles were dying, too. No one knows just why this happened. Reptiles are cold-blooded. That means their blood cannot be warmer than the air around them. It may have become too cold for the reptiles. And the cold was killing the plants they ate. The dinosaurs all died. Now only the fossils of those mighty monsters are left. But a new kind of animal appeared to take the place of the giants.

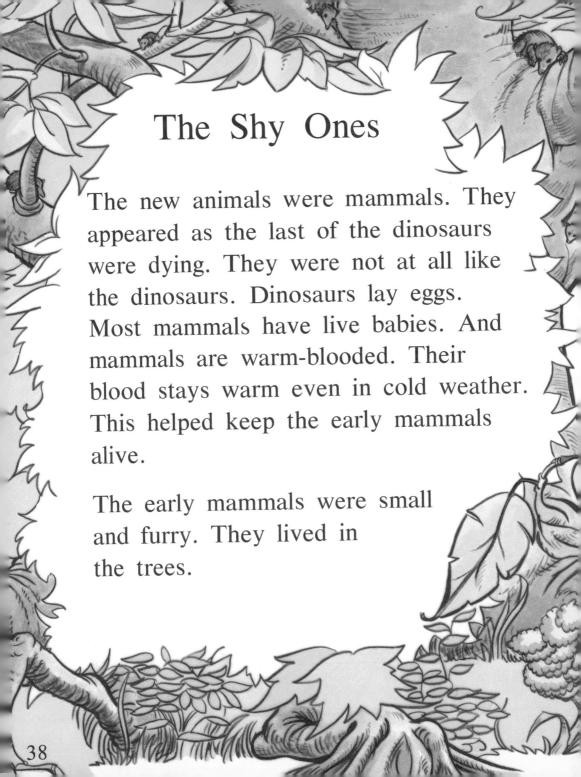

The Shy Ones

The new animals were mammals. They appeared as the last of the dinosaurs were dying. They were not at all like the dinosaurs. Dinosaurs lay eggs. Most mammals have live babies. And mammals are warm-blooded. Their blood stays warm even in cold weather. This helped keep the early mammals alive.

The early mammals were small and furry. They lived in the trees.

They ate fruits, seeds and insects.
And dinosaur eggs were a tasty snack—
if they could find them. Sometimes a
little mammal left his tree home. First
he would peek out through the leaves.
If no one was around he might come
out. He had to be careful. The shy
little mammal would have been a tasty
snack for a dinosaur.

The Hidden Horse

The air on land was becoming warmer.
There were more trees. Great forests
covered the land. The first horses
lived in these forests. They were not
like the horses we see today. The first
horses were no bigger than dogs! They
did not have hoofs as horses do now.
Each of their hind legs had three toes.
Each front leg had four. The first
horses could not run fast. So they had
to hide from their enemies. They hid
among the many trees. They ate the
leaves on the low branches.
They were too short to
reach anything higher.

As time passed, the small furry horses grew taller and larger. Their eyes got bigger. So did their teeth. And so did their brains. Their many toes turned into one strong hoof. Their necks became longer. They could bend down to eat grass. All these changes were good for them. Because they were able to change, horses did not die out.

The world was still changing, too. Many of the trees died. The horses began to live in open country. There was no place for them to hide. The only way to get away from their enemies was to run—fast! Those little horses in the woods were the "grandfathers" of today's great runners.

The   Peaceful Monster

The Beast of Baluchistan (buh-LOO-ki-stan) was the biggest mammal that ever lived on land. He lived millions of years ago. He was an early member of the rhinoceros family. But he didn't have a horn on his head as rhinos do now. He did not need a horn to fight his enemies. He didn't need anything. He was so huge, other animals stayed away from him. But he was peaceful. All he wanted to do was eat.

The Beasts of Baluchistan didn't eat meat. They ate plants and leaves. The Beasts needed a lot of food to fill their big stomachs. They could eat up a whole forest in a few days. Then they had to find more food. They walked slowly along from tree to tree. It was hard for them to move. And they had to stop often to eat. On soft ground they were in trouble. They might sink into the squishy mud. And they might not be able to get out. They would flounder around until they died. The biggest land mammal ever didn't always have an easy life.

The Camels Are Coming

Many things happened about the
time the Beasts of Baluchistan were
dying out. There were great floods.
A lot of trees died. Inside the earth
there were explosions. The explosions
pushed up great rocks and huge chunks
of land. That was how many mountains
were made. The air turned cooler.
More trees died from the cold.
Now there were not as many
forests. But there were more
and more animals.

One of the early members of the camel
family lived then. He was Alticamelus
(all-tee-come-EE-lus). He could run fast
on his long thin legs. He ran so fast,
it was hard for other animals to catch
him. He had two small sharp hoofs on
each foot. Today, camels have big flat
feet. They need them to walk on sandy
deserts. But Alticamelus didn't live on
a sandy desert. He lived on the plains
in North America. There were trees
and grass for him to eat. That was
lucky for him. Camels of today store fat
in their humps. But early Alticamelus
probably didn't have a hump. He didn't
need one.

Tusk-Tusk

Most of us have seen elephants. But we have never seen one that looked like a Trilophodon (try-LUFF-o-don). He was a very early member of the elephant family. Like most elephants, Trilophodons had tusks. But they had two sets of tusks! The tusks in their upper jaws were very long front teeth. And they had two more tusks in their long lower jaws.

The Trilophodons roamed together in
herds. They could defend themselves
better when they were together. As
they roamed, they looked for food.
Those double tusks helped them dig
up grass and plants. Many plants and
trees that grew then are almost the
same as those that are growing today.
And the land that the Trilophodons
walked on millions of years ago is still
here. But the Trilophodons, and the
other amazing monsters of
long ago, are gone.

The Killer Cat

Lions and tigers and cats belong to the feline family. A long-ago cousin of theirs was Smiladon (SMILE-o-don). He was the most terrible "cat" that ever lived. He is called Sabre-Tooth because of his two front teeth. They were long and sharp and looked like daggers. When Smiladon attacked, he stabbed his teeth right into his victim's neck. He stabbed and stabbed until his prey died.

Then he used his sharp teeth to slice up the dead body. But he couldn't chew because his teeth were too long. They stuck out and got in the way. That didn't matter to Smiladon. He opened his mouth wide and his lower jaw dropped. Then he was able to swallow whole chunks in a gulp.

Smiladon's nose was far back on his head. When he sank his teeth into an animal, the fur didn't get into his nose. Smiladon was able to breathe while he killed. All the Smiladons died out thousands of years ago. That's a good thing. A Smiladon was cruel even when he was a kitten.

The Death Trap

Smiladon fossils were found at the La
Brea Tar Pits in California not very
long ago. Thousands of years ago the
pits were full of soft black tar. The
tar was covered with water. Animals
used to wander by the pits. Maybe a
Trilophodon stopped. As he drank, he
sank into the sticky tar. He tried and
tried to get out. A Smiladon came along.
He jumped on the Trilophodon to eat
him. Now both monsters were trapped.
A bird flew over them. He attacked
Smiladon. Then all three were stuck
and sinking. They soon died.

After many years the soft tar became hard. Whatever had been trapped in the tar turned into fossils. When people discovered the Tar Pits they found many fossils. They dug up fossils of camels, horses, snakes, mice, deer, turtles, birds, and many other creatures.

Today there is a museum at the Tar Pits. You can see all the fossils. Now it is safe to visit the Trap of Death.

The Great Freeze

Year after year it grew colder and colder. In many places the world was covered with fields of thick white ice. These fields are called glaciers. Some of those glaciers are still there. They are all that is left of the Ice Ages. The cold was terrible then. Some animals kept moving, trying to find a warm place. Some animals grew coats of thick hair. Some learned to live in caves. Many died. But if the animals lived through the cold, they had a new enemy to fear—Man.

Meet the People

The first people who lived on earth did not look like anybody we know. Their bodies were covered with thick hair like the animals'. But even the earliest people were smarter than other animals. For one thing, they learned how to make fire. Fire kept people warm. The early people learned to make tools and weapons out of stone. They used the weapons to kill animals for food. They used the tools to skin the animals. Those skins were the first clothes.

The early people moved from place to place together. They were safer that way. They could defend and help each other. The early men and women were able to think. So they stayed alive through the hard, cold Ice Ages.

By the end of the last Ice Age people were wiser and stronger. They had learned to do many things. And they would learn to do even more. The Age of Man had begun.

Clumsy Creature

Megatherium (meg-a-THEER-ee-um) was
a giant sloth. He lived during the Ice
Ages. He was as big as an elephant.
He crawled slowly on the outside
edges of his feet. As he went
along, he ate grass and plants.
The early people might have
seen this strange monster.
But he probably did
not bother them.
Megatherium was
a gentle giant if
he was left alone.

The Swinger

The Glyptodont (GLIP-toe-dont) was a giant armadillo. He had a shell like a turtle. But what a shell the Glyptodont had!

It was very tough and had a high hump in the middle. The shell helped to keep a Glyptodont safe from his enemies. Some Glyptodonts even had shells on their heads.

Some Glyptodonts had strange tails.
There were balls of sharp spikes on
the ends of the tails. A Glyptodont
could swing his tail like a club.
He could use it to attack an enemy.
The early people might have met a
Glyptodont. If they did, they probably
kept away from him—and that
spiky, swinging tail.

The Big Woollies

The Woolly Rhino was almost as big as the Beast of Baluchistan. They were both members of the rhino family. But the peaceful Woolly Rhino lived many years after the Beast of Baluchistan. The Woolly Rhino lived during the Ice Ages. His coat of long dark fur kept him warm in the terrible cold. The Woolly Rhino's fur kept the early people warm, too. They hunted Woolly Rhinos for their thick coats and for food.

Man also hunted other huge animals—
the Woolly Mammoths (MAM-muths).
Their shaggy fur made fine rugs, as well
as warm clothes. The Woolly Mammoth
was a member of the elephant family. He
had a trunk and great twisted tusks.
The mammoth had two humps. One was
on his back. The other was on his head.
A strange place for a hump! He stored
fat in his humps. He used that fat when
he couldn't find anything to eat.

In a museum in Russia there is a stuffed mammoth. He was found frozen in the ice. He had been there for thousands of years. He almost fell apart when he was taken out. But his skin was saved. He is half-sitting now, just as he was when he died so long ago.

Thousands of years ago people drew pictures of mammoths. They drew them on the walls of their caves. Some of the pictures can be seen today.

It has been a very long time since any-
one has seen a living mammoth. There
are none left now. Once, people needed
the mammoths. And they hunted them.
But now all those marvelous giants
are gone.

The Last of the Giants

Once, the world was full of enormous
animals. Now they are gone. All the
dinosaurs died. The huge mammals, like
the Beasts of Baluchistan, are no more.
But the biggest animals that have ever
lived—the blue whales—are still here.

A blue whale can weigh as much as 187
tons. Brachiosaurus, the largest of all
the dinosaurs, weighed only 50 tons.

Whales ruled the sea from prehistoric times until only a few hundred years ago. Then men began to hunt them. Whales are easy to find. Most of the time they swim close to the top of the water. They have to dive down into the deep water for food. But they always come back to the top to breathe. As they breathe, they blow out a great stream of air and water. This shows the hunters just where the whale is. Whales are strong and clever. They have no trouble getting away from their fish enemies. But they don't seem to learn that men can be dangerous.

There are many kinds of whales. Some of them have "songs." The songs of the white whales sound like whistles or squeaks. Other songs sound like creaks or clicks or bangs or beeps. We hope the songs of the whales will never end. But people are still killing whales. Unless they stop, all the whales will soon be gone. We can't let this happen to the whales. We must take care of the world's last giants . . . and all the other wonderful creatures who share the earth with us.

WHITE
WHALE

LEONORA & ARTHUR HORNBLOW are the co-authors of the popular and unique Step-Up natural-history books.

Arthur Hornblow, Jr. is best known as the movie producer who made such famous films as *Oklahoma, Weekend at the Waldorf, Gaslight* and *Witness for the Prosecution.*

Leonora Hornblow is a columnist, novelist, and author of historical books for children.

The Hornblows live in New York City where they are Associate Members of the American Museum of Natural History and the New York Zoological Society.

MICHAEL K. FRITH went to Harvard, where he spent most of his time writing and drawing for the Harvard Lampoon. Since then he has spent most of his time writing and/or drawing for even younger children: *The Perils of Penelope* (a Sesame Street Book), *My Amazing Book of... Autographs!* and *Some of Us Walk, Some Fly, Some Swim* (Beginner Books), *I'll Teach My Dog 100 Words* (a Bright and Early Book), and all of the Hornblows' nature books. He and his family live in New York.